Press Kit Swiyyah Woodard

ISBN-13 : 978-1979968614

www.dontcallmecrazy.com Call (727) 280-5607;swiyyah@dontcallmecrazy.com

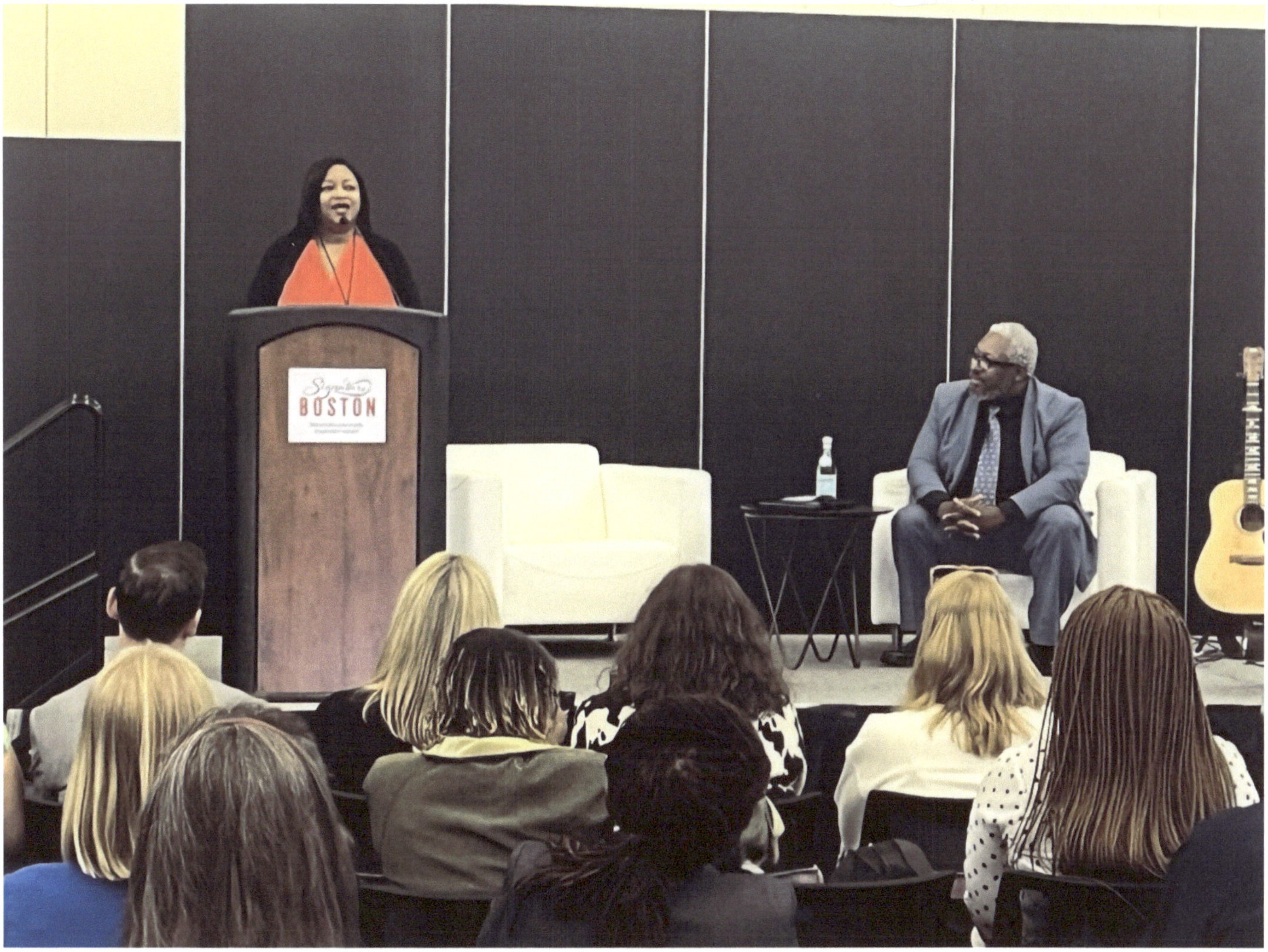

I was born in the projects of Bethel Heights listening to gun fire almost every night. In my earliest years, I felt a sense of protection because I had my dad by my side. But then at the age of 3 my parents divorced and I had to be raised in a single parent home. At the age of five my brother molested me. I forgave him because I knew a young girl did the same to him.

By the time I entered school, I had slurred speech and didn't care to make friends, so I was often bullied by my peers. A young girl wanted to fight me so I decided to take my own life at the age of eight. I looked into the medicine cabinet for medication to take but I could not find any.

My mother remarried and I ended up being physically abused by my step dad. The abuse was so severe that God blocked it from my memory. At the age of only 23 the brother that molested me committed suicide. This was very devastating to me and my entire family. I didn't want to give up hope.

I had dreams and goals so with my mother's encouraging words I went on to college and received my BA degree in Psychology. This was the proudest moment in my life. I felt like I could concur the world, and had no idea of the trauma that would soon unfold.

It took a year to find a job but I found one in the field of mental health. I hated the way the therapist used to talk about the patients in the break room, naming names and telling of their patient's life tragedies.

One therapist said, "This child's file is so thick there's no hope for him." It was also very stressful going from one client's house to another hearing about their severe family problems. I quit that job to find another one and this was the start of my downward spiral.

I started seeing faces everywhere. There were faces in the sheets, faces in the walls. I began getting migraine headaches everyday for six months. I began having racing thoughts, delusions, hallucinations. I started talking to myself, laughing, and crying, all at the same time.

I was then Baker Acted. The doctors sat me down, looked me in the eye, and said, "You have the most debilitating mental illness known in mental health, paranoid schizophrenia." I felt I was normal. I never had any disciplinary problems in school and I made good grades so I refused the medication and was hospitalized six times.

My family took a picture of me at my worst and that's when I knew I needed help.

I've been taking medication now for seven years without a relapse. During my first episode God told me that a movie would be made about me and I would later become wealthy. At the time, I didn't have a job, a car, or any money but I had faith that one day his revelation would come to light.

And today I have actual offers from directors who want to produce a movie about my book, which is now required reading for a class at St. Petersburg College.

My message is that through God, any dream is possible. He has a dream for you bigger than what you can imagine. One of the keys to success that I highlight in my book is to "walk by faith." Begin living out your dreams. Do what you love for free, and then start reading books, exploring your field, and cultivating a way to make a living by doing what you love.

Everyone has gifts. It's up to you to discover your God-given talent. And remember, life is 1% what happens to you, and 99% how your react to it. Never give up!

Swiyyah Muhammad is the author of *Don't Call Me Crazy! I'm Just in Love* and a motivational speaker. She was recognized as a Bay News 9 Everyday Hero last year, and has been profiled by several local media. To reach Swiyyah visit **www. dontcallmecrazy.com or call 727-776-0291.**

COMMUNI

Local Author Fair

ST. PETERSBURG - Mark your calendar, for Saturday, Jan, 7 from 11 a.m. to 3 p.m. Authors from all over the Tampa Bay area will be providing a free hour of "Don't Call Me Crazy! I'm Just in Love." The event will take place at the Main Library at 3745 9th Ave. N., St. Petersburg.

Swiyyah said, "I wrote my book to end the stigma on mental illness and to help the community grow mentally, spiritually and financially. It took me two years to get my books into the public library system. I'm reaching all my goals and I want to help the community reach all of their goals."

"57 million Americans will suffer from a mental disorder this year and only 13 percent of them will seek treatment. Thirty thousand lives are lost each year because people are afraid to seek help. They're afraid to be labeled as crazy. My brother committed suicide. If I had known the warning signs I could have saved his life," she continued. "Don't Call Me Crazy! I'm Just in Love" teaches the warning signs of mental illness."

Swiyyah Nadirah Muhammad received her BA in Psychology and has also been diagnosed with the most debilitating mental illness known in mental health, paranoid schizophrenia. For a long time she refused to take any medication. "I always saw myself as normal and I thought that normal people don't get mental illnesses. I was stereotyping the disorder, which is what a lot of people do. I

Swiyyah Muhammad

learned later that 49 percent of Americans will experience a mental disorder at least once in their lives," Swiyyah said.

Swiyyah wants to reach out to the community. For more information visit her website, www.SWIYYAH.com.

The Weekly Challenger

We Value *Diversity* | We Value *Education* | We Value *History*

VOL. 48 NO. 15　　DECEMBER 3 - DECEMBER 9, 2015　　50¢

Log on to TheWeeklyChallenger.com

For Sports, Money Tips, Beyond the Bay, Recipes and much more!

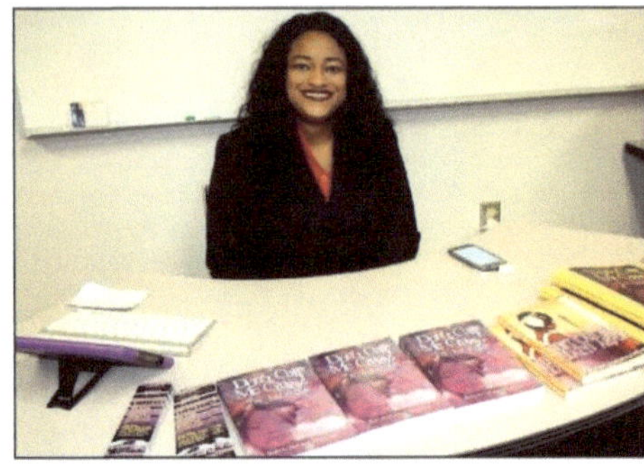

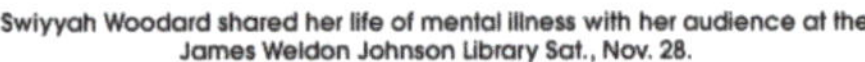

Swiyyah Woodard shared her life of mental illness with her audience at the James Weldon Johnson Library Sat., Nov. 28.

From a mental institution to helping others

BY CINDY CARTER
Staff Writer

ST. PETERSBURG –Swiyyah Nadirah Woodard has spent a lifetime trying to overcome one struggle after another. But with friends, family and modern medicine on her side, she has made miraculous breakthroughs and is embarking on a life full of positivity and success.

Her beginnings are recognizable to those familiar with tragedy. When Woodard was just three years old her father walked out, leaving her mom to raise both her and her siblings. At the age of five, she was molested by her brother, and later physically abused by her mother's new husband.

"The abuse was so severe that God blocked it from my memory," explained Woodard who has spent a lifetime coming to terms with it.

Unfortunately Woodard's trouble didn't stop there. In school she recalled being bullied, mostly because of her slurred speech, and retreated into herself. At eight she wanted to kill herself. Her only saving grace was that she couldn't find any medication laying around the house to take.

Her world was yet to fall apart completely. While in his early 20s, the brother that molested her committed suicide, further tearing apart her life and that of her family. Encouraged by her mother to open a new chapter in her life, she attended college earning a bachelor's degree in psychology.

"I had no idea of the trauma that was to unfold," said Woodard to the group of listeners at the James Weldon Johnson Library, eager to grab hold of her new book entitled, "Don't Call Me Crazy Again," a sequel to her 2007 debut "Don't Call Me Crazy," which is required reading at St. Petersburg College and some high schools in courses dealing with mental health.

The trauma she was referring to was her being diagnosed as a paranoid schizophrenic. At 28, her life was turned upside down. Woodard had just started her second job working in a mental health facility: "This was the start of my downward spiral," she said.

Her symptoms were quite extreme. First she started seeing faces everywhere. "There were faces in the walls, in the rugs, in the sheets," said Woodard. Migraine headaches came next followed by racing thoughts, hallucinations and delusions.

She was hospitalized countless times, prescribed medication to control her symptoms, medication she refused to take.

"I didn't believe it," she said. Woodard remembers studying Abnormal Psychology in class and her picture of someone with schizophrenia seemed the opposite of herself.

She never had disciplinary problems in school and she made decent grades, so she didn't consider herself ill. It wasn't until after her sixth hospitalization that she realized she was in trouble. Cocaine was found in her system and she couldn't remember how it had gotten there, her lungs collapsed twice.

"My sister took a picture of me at my worst, that's when I knew I needed help," said Woodard.

For the past eight years Woodard has kept herself out of a relapse by faithfully taking her medication and practicing positivity. She immediately started writing, to get it all out and because she wanted people who are struggling with mental illness or those caring for them to know they aren't alone.

"Sharing a story helps to end the stigma," Woodard said to her audience encouraging them to share their own experiences with mental illness.

At 39, Woodard is now a motivational speaker who hopes her life's ordeal will inspire people to go after their dreams regardless of their disability or lot in life.

"I believe through God any dream is possible, and I'm living proof," she said.

Woodard encourages others to find what they love to do for free, get better at it even if it takes years to perfect their skills and create a business doing what they love. "You have to take baby steps," she said. "You can't be fooled by the get rich quick schemes."

Over the years Woodard has worked to become a better person; she strives to handle her interactions with others better, to love a little harder. In addition, she writes a lot of to-do-lists and spends time visualizing her success. Something she said everyone should do regardless of whether they have a mental illness or not.

"I see a lot of talented people who will go hard for two years and if they don't see the results they're expecting, they quit," said Woodard. She feels if you don't lose faith and stick with what you love, eventually your dreams will take off and lead to success. "You want to keep going."

Woodard wrapped up her motivational talk with food and drink and the opportunity for others to buy her books. But above, all her wish for the event was not to sell a bunch of books, but to provide others with tangible information if dealing with a mental health issue, and to know all is not lost.

"Counselors said I was crazy, I'd never be successful and I should be stuck in a mental institution for the rest of my life," finished Woodard. "Well I proved them wrong."

If you think you or someone you love may have a mental illness, Woodard suggests getting help from somewhere. Talking to others can help unburden the soul and lead to positivity that will essentially transform life.

To find out more about Woodard and how to purchase her books, log onto dontcallmecrazy.com.

---

48 Years of Service to the Tampa Bay Area • www.TheWeeklyChallenger.com • 727-896-2922

Pre-Thanksgiving food basket giveaway

Princess Denise Wright

Rashida Strober

Swiyyah Muhammad

ST. PETERSBURG — Radio host Princess Denise Wright of Praise 1590 AM and 96.5 FM, and Matters of the Heart Ministry will host a Pre-Thanksgiving Food Basket Giveaway for needy families this Sat., Nov. 10 from 11 a.m. to 1 p.m.

Located at Glad Tidings Assembly of God, 4200 17th Ave N. in St. Petersburg, the event will include praise and worship by Derrick Isham, author Swiyyah Muhammad, playwright/actress Rashida Strober, and other anointed entertainment.

The African American Women's Author Showcase has teamed up with Matters of the Heart Ministry to raise funds and seek donations of non perishable food items for needy families during the Thanksgiving and Christmas holidays.

The showcase will feature award winning author of "Don't Call Me Crazy! I'm Just in Love," Swiyyah Muhammad. The book tells her story of overcoming a debilitating mental disorder, and how she strives to help others to overcome also. She is on a mission to end the stigma of mental illness.

Muhammad has traveled the United States spreading the word, and her book is now required reading at St. Petersburg College. She offers hope, love and care to those who are in the situation she was once in.

Award winning actress Rashida Strober will perform a character from her play "A Dark Skinned Woman's Revenge." The play is about five dark-skinned women and how the color of their skin impacts their relationships with men.

Everyone is invited to come out and support this wonderful humanitarian community event that will give hope and love to so many in need during these hard economic times.

Local sponsors are Walmart, Sweetbay, Walgreens, Publix, Praise 1590 WRXB, LaRocca Chiropractic, Sister to Sisters Ministry.

If you would like to be a sponsor or donate food items, please contact Princess Denise Wright at (727) 412-4925. Registration is required for all needy families.

About Swiyyah Woodard:

Swiyyah Woodard is CEO of Swiyyah Productions Inc. and Baynews9 Everyday Hero, seen by 2 million viewers. She began training as an actor at the age of 13. She was then accepted into the PCCA program at Gibbs high school for the giftedly talented in acting. She obtained a BA degree in Psychology from the University of South Florida, and is certified in Creative Writing and TV production. The first TV show that she produced was entitled, "Living my dreams," and aired in 200,000 households. She featured platinum and gold selling artist such as Rick Ross, Khia, and DJ Trans. After receiving her BA degree, Swiyyah, was hospitalized 6 times and diagnosed with paranoid schizophrenia. As a child she was raised in poverty with a single parent, molested by her brother, abused by her step dad, thought of suicide at the age of 8, lost the brother that molested her to suicide, and in her early 30's, her lungs collapsed twice. She felt the strong need to tell her story and published two books inspired by her true story entitled, "Don't Call Me Crazy!" Her first book became required and suggested reading at an accredited 4-year University in Writing, Reading, Abnormal and General Psychology.

She was awarded thousands from a rehabilitation service to start her speaking and production business. She has spoken for Macy*s call center, Universities, the public school system, churches, and many other organizations. She raised money through sponsorships and grants to put on various mental health awareness events throughout the community. A few being "MLK Day of Service grant," with SPC college, sponsorship to buy books from Central Florida Behavior Network, and support from Walmart. She was recognized and featured as a Baynews9 Everyday Hero, seen by two million viewers and a Tampa Bay Black Girl that rocks. She also collaborates with the Federation of Families of Florida Inc. to put on community events. Swiyyah's books are fictional inspired by her true story and written in a self-help format.

Don't Call Me Crazy! I'm Just in Love
A Novel by Swiyyah Woodard

The two main characters in this book are named Anika and Mosi. Their love for one another is strong and will surpass anything, even schizophrenia.

Anika, in the middle of the story, is diagnosed with the most debilitating disorder known in mental health, paranoid schizophrenia. She has breaks from reality, paranoid hallucinations, disorganized speech, and no one including the doctors can figure out the cause. This book has been written in order to identify signs of mental distress for those readers that may be at risk of having a break from reality, being involuntarily baker acted, to change misconceived stereotypes associated with schizophrenia, and to teach mental health professionals how to treat mentally ill clients.

Anika also throughout the book is in search of religion, true Religion. She was born into Islam but never studied this religion or any other religion. The characters in this book unknowingly assist her in finding an understanding of God; the professor of the University that she attends, the other man, Mosi, and her mother. The other man is named David, who she meets in the beginning of the chapters. David is an attractive man who tries to introduce her to religion and in doing so falls deeply in love with her. But she remains faithful to her boyfriend and as a result breaks the heart of David, causing David to develop an eerie obsession for her. Her mother has the strongest unshakeable faith in God. When Anika is headed down the wrong paths in life her mother is always there to give her words of wisdom and guides her towards true happiness.

This book is appealing to several types of readers. It has been written on three different levels, appealing to three different types of audiences. The first level can appeal to all readers that enjoy romance novels. The second level will appeal to those who are educated in subjects of Parapsychology and Abnormal psychology. The third level of this book will appeal to those in tune with their own spirituality.

About the Author:
Swiyyah Nadirah Woodard received her BA degree in Psychology with a concentration in Business Administration. Her book is now required reading at SPC College. She resides in Saint Petersburg Florida and loves her city. Learn more at www.dontcallmecrazy.com

---

1st edition soft cover: ISBN: 978-0-9889457-0-8 Retail: 14.99 USD Price-encoded EAN Barcode* Dimensions: 5.5 x 8.5 194 pgs
Young Adult and Adult Fiction. Ages 13 and up, and adults of all ages.
Release:January 2007 Published by: Swiyyah Productions Inc.

Clients

- SPC College
- Pinellas County Schools
- Central Connecticut State University

  Macy*s Call Center

- **BMS**
- Pinellas County Urban League
- **This Is My Brave**
- Saint Petersburg Islamic Center
- Matters of the Heart Ministry
- Candy Lowe Tea Time
- Word Power Publications

- Faith Denominational Atscolic Church
- Atlanta Black Theatre Festival
- Tampa Black Heritage Festival
- Public Library Saint Petersburg, FL
- Johnson Branch Library Saint Petersburg, FL
- African American Authors Showcase
- Igbobia Church Gospel Foundation Inc.
- Five Star Events
- Juneteenth Pinellas County

A TRIUMPH OVER MENTAL ILLNESS

Special guest: Swiyyah Woodard, Mental Health Expert, Foremost Authority on Mental Illness and Author of "Don't Call Me Crazy! I'm Just in Love"

Swiyyah Woodard survived a debilitating mental illness. Learn how she worked herself well to become a community hero.

Swiyyah Woodard can discuss this by answering the following questions:

- How does mental illness affect someone?
- What advice do you have for people to heal from mental illness?
- Is getting past prejudice and stigma towards the mentally ill often more difficult than the symptoms themselves?
- Can people still live out their dreams despite having a mental illness? How?
- What does her book cover regarding mental illness?

Meet Swiyyah Woodard:

-Received her BA degree in Psychology from the University of South FL
-Diagnosed as a schizophrenic
-Expert on Mental Health
-Author of "Don't Call Me Crazy! I'm Just in Love"

For more information visit

www.dontcallmecrazy.com Call (727) 280-5607;swiyyah@dontcallmecrazy.com

Awards and Certifications

University of South Florida

has conferred on

Swiyyah Nadirah Muhammad

the degree of

Bachelor of Arts

together with all the rights, privileges and honors appertaining thereto in consideration
of the satisfactory completion of the course prescribed by the Faculty of the

College of Arts and Sciences

In Witness Thereof the undersigned have affixed their names and the seal of the University

at Tampa, Florida, this tenth day of August, 2001.

University of South Florida
St. Petersburg

Swiyyah Woodard

has completed all requirements for the certificate program in

Creative Writing

prescribed by the

College of Arts and Sciences

In Witness Thereof the undersigned have affixed their names and the seal of the University

at St. Petersburg, Florida, this fifth day of May, 2017.

Regional Chancellor

Dean, College of Arts and Sciences

<u>Letters of Recommendation</u>

SPC ST. PETERSBURG COLLEGE

SOCIAL AND BEHAVIORAL SCIENCES
Clearwater Campus
727-791-5963

November 1, 2013

Dear Swiyyah:

Thank you for speaking with Saint Petersburg College students on October 18, 2013. We offer to you our sincerest gratitude. Your presentation sparked compelling academic discussions with both General Psychology and Abnormal Psychology students. Thank you also for taking time to carefully and thoughtfully respond to the questions asked by each student. You provided students with a pathway to receive authentic feedback regarding the complexities and eventual benefits of enduring the symptoms of schizophrenia.

Your presentation also served to motivate those that attended. Your honesty and openness came from a source of strength. This letter extends to you our sincerest gratitude.

Sincerely,

Ada Timmons Ward, Ed.D
Psychology Professor
Social and Behavioral Sciences

Kim Molinaro
Psychology Professor
Social and Behavioral Sciences

Pinellas County Urban League, Inc.

Building for Equal Opportunity

333 – 31st Street North
St. Petersburg, FL 33713

Phone: (727) 327-2081
Fax: (727) 321-8349

Web Site: www.pcul.org
E-Mail: info@pcul.org

September 21, 2011

Ms. Swiyyah Muhammad
P. O. Box 12706
St. Petersburg, FL 33733

Dear Ms. Muhammad:

Thank you for participating as an expert speaker and community vendor during our recent 27th Annual Crime Prevention Run & Family Festival. Your participation added a lot to our event and we look forward to working with you again in the future.

We are particularly grateful for you generous contribution to the Pinellas County Urban League. By assisting us, you contribute to our programming, research and advocacy that empowers our community and changes lives. Your gift of $ 5.00 may be a tax-deductible donation because we are a 501 (c) 3 designated corporation. You may wish to consult a tax advisor for more details.

Please continue to keep me as an active contact in your networking file. Please feel free to call on me when I may assist you in your endeavors. Best wishes, always!

Sincerely,

Michael O. Adekunle
Crime Prevention Program

Supported By:

AFFILIATED WITH THE NATIONAL URBAN LEAGUE, INC.

To Whom It May Concern:

I am endorsing the book, Don't Call Me Crazy- I'm Just in Love by SPC alumni Swiyyah Muhammad. The book is a narration that reveals the journey of a young woman's challenge with mental illness. The novel helps us explore the complex nature of a paranoid schizophrenia forcing us to think more deeply about the stigmatism imposed upon mental illness. The novel allows students to place themselves at the heart of this societal issue connecting it with their own lives and developing a voice about its negative connotation; an issue we know very little about.

The book was used in (4) Developmental Reading courses and (1) Developmental Writing course and was the subject of our online discussion forum. Ms.Muhammad was invited as a guest speaker to inspire students to read more outside of class and the objective was to provide practice in applying the comprehension strategies learned in class.

Ms.Muhammad's outstanding presentation built anticipation and excitement to read her book. As she discussed the characters, she validated her story as she revealed the issues of her life. Students felt comfortable enough to talk about their mental illness and other issues never talked about before.

Angela Sweet
Adjunct Faculty
Developmental
Reading
Communications-
SPC Gibbs
727-768-3999

<u>Photos of Events</u>

Atlanta Black Theatre Festival

Car Wrap

Life coach
Husband; Dederick

Fan appreciation

Fans of Swiyyah

Fan of Swiyyah

Saint Petersburg College

Saint Petersburg Public Library

African American Author's Showcase

Raising money for children in Africa

Matters of the heart Ministry

Play Wright Rashida Strober Radio

Faith Denominational Atscolic Church

Charity Ball Tampa

Fan of Swiyyah Tampa

Fan of Swiyyah

Fan of Swiyyah

Memorabilia

Baynews9 Everyday Hero

Tampa Bay Black Heritage Festival

Bill Murphy reporter Baynews9

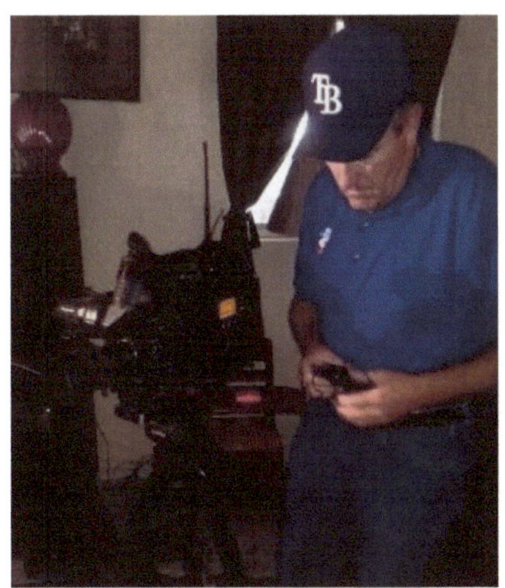

Camera man Baynews9

First National TV show

Raising Money for hospital patient

WRXB Radio Maurice Sebation

Sponsor Steve Manning

Raising money for Suicide Prevention

Don't Call
Me Crazy!
I'm Just in Love
SWIYYAH NADIRAH WOODARD

Don't Call
Me Crazy!
Again
SWIYYAH NADIRAH WOODARD

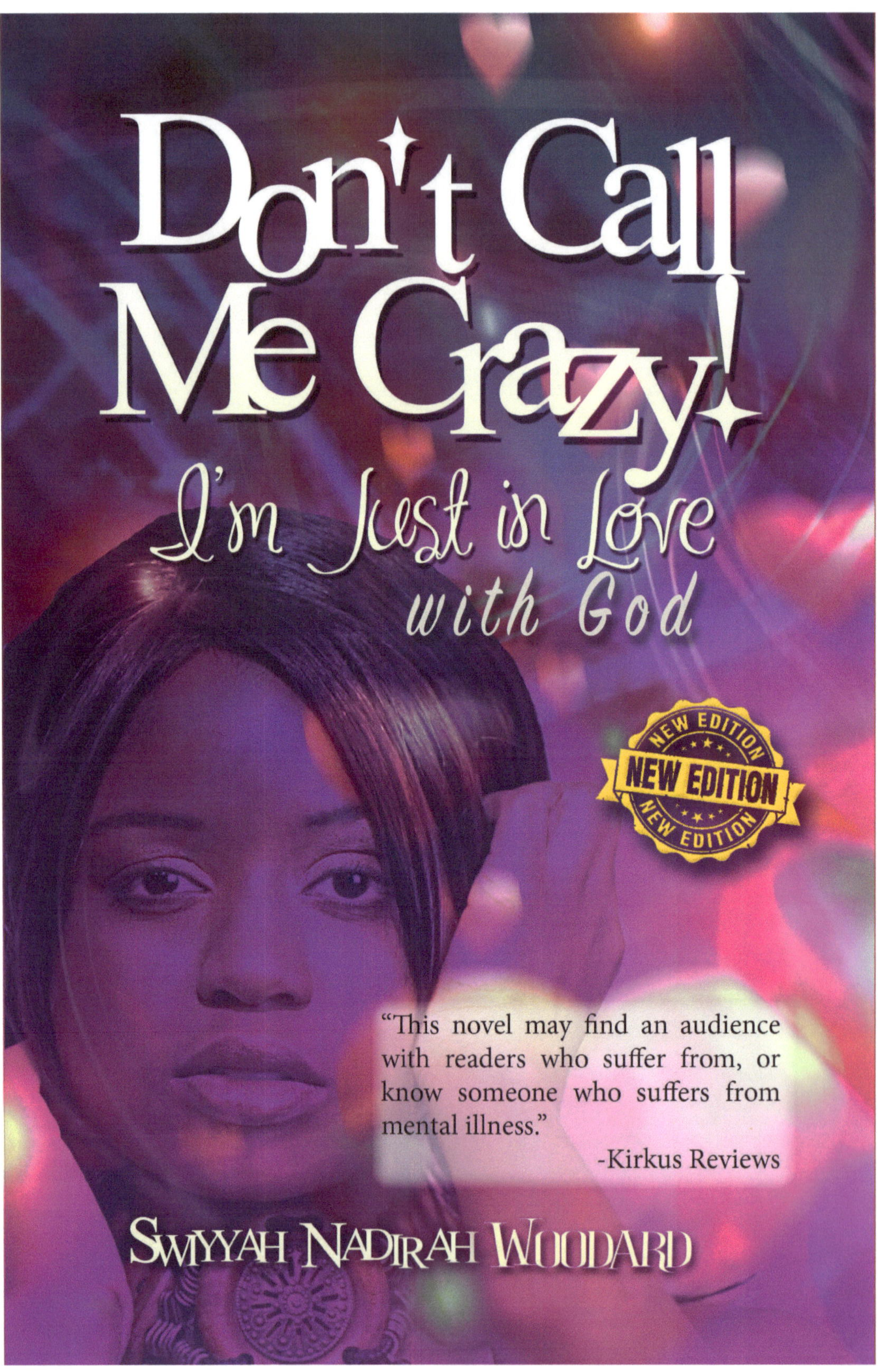

Don't Call Me Crazy!
I'm Just in Love with God
NEW EDITION
"This novel may find an audience with readers who suffer from, or know someone who suffers from mental illness."
-Kirkus Reviews
SWIYYAH NADIRAH WOODARD

HELPING TO END THE STIGMA OF MENTAL ILLNESS
SWIYYAH WOODARD
LET'S BE
Inspired
Undefeated Despite Schizophrenia

Free Book Sample: Don't Call Me Crazy! I'm Just in Love

"Mom, I'm so upset and embarrassed. Mary made me look like a fool in

front of her friends, telling them how I've been with Mosi for eight years

and telling me that I should dump him. I'm not going to listen to her advice,

I love that man," Anika says.

Her mother sits up straight in her seat.

"You must know who you are and your purpose in life so you will not be

so affected by what others say. You must learn how to solve your own problems. One of the reasons I don't give advice is because it might come back to bite you if it's not what they want to hear. Besides, most people want you to just listen to them when they have a problem instead of telling them what to do. And, I try to stay away from drama at all cost."

"What do you mean, drama?" Anika questions with a perplexed look on her face trying to fit the puzzle pieces of Ms. Muhammad's teaching.

"Drama," the mother explains, "is characterized by a lot of things. Number one, just as in your situation, when everything is going well, a person who enjoys digging up past pains and traumas in order to have for themselves a dramatic excitable conversation will do just that. The friend may feel as if they are helping you come to the right decision, even though only you are the only one who can make the right decisions for you. Number two, pay attention to who your friends are and which family members you get along with best. Nine times out of ten, we choose to surround ourselves around people that compliment us. If we want drama, we hang around negative individuals; if we want happiness and success, we hang around positive people. Think about it. Number three, sometimes when we have a fear of making our own decisions we push others into making decisions for us. An example being, if a person asks how you are doing, say, 'I am doing just fine.' If they ask how you are doing and your reply is to tell them every last bad thing that has happen to you within the last week, that gives the drama-stricken people the opportunity to engage in negativity. You want to stay away from negativity at all cost. I don't even watch dramatic programs on television. Negativity and the inability to solve your own problems as an adult, sometimes bring about depression. We all experience depression at one time or another, but some people experience it all the time and if that's the case, they must ask themselves why it occurs."

"Well, I'm always depressed and I need to know why," Anika says.

Anika's mother offers advice, "Depression for me, comes from a lack of freedom. I'd like to be free to utilize my natural-born talents to engage in activities that help others, but I'm too busy working nine to five. The secret is to work full-time for as long as it takes you to save money to start a business, and utilize your talents to help others. Then go down to part-time. You have to set goals and visualize yourself reaching them. Share your goals only with people who want to see you succeed. Taking risks is a part of becoming the person you want to be."

"That makes a lot of sense," her mother's daughter sits attentively, focusing on the knowledge imparted to her.

Anika's mother continues, "Depression also stems from stress and the inability to control your life. You have to be in control of your own life and be able to face life head on. Some people run to the bottle or drugs when a problem arises; they drink or smoke, but once they come down from their high they're faced with the same problems. It's best to just face life and find ways to jump over those obstacles that we face. Know that we are tested daily and have the tools necessary to rise above it all. Learn to love life. Love the fight, love the small things that we are blessed to have and experience. Love yourself. This is how to develop spiritually," Anika's mother says with confidence.